I don't know who you are but I love you

Connecting with Your Loved One
Despite the Fog of Dementia

An informative book full of helpful tips on how to keep communication lines open and still enjoy the bonds of relationship with your loved ones diagnosed with dementia.

Regardless of the stage of illness, Nela Allan offers concrete actions and steps to guide you to create visits enjoyable on both sides making it easy to keep coming back.

Written by
Nela Allan

Illustrations by
Robert Allan

Published by Nela Allan

Copyright © Nela Allan, 2019

ISBN: 978-0-646-81059-1

Publisher: Nela Allan

This book is written with the heartfelt intent to provide helpful and informative material on the subjects addressed in the publication. The opinions, experience and ideas found within are that of its author. Even though the steps outlined in this book are presented to assist you to move forward with the goals of communication there is no guarantee that these will be achieved by reading this book. The author of this book does not dispense medical advice nor prescribe the use of any technique as a form of treatment for physical, emotional, or medical problems without the advice of a physician, either directly or indirectly. The intent of the author is to offer information of a general nature to help you in your communications with a loved one with Dementia. In the event that you use any of the information in this book for yourself, the author and publisher assume no responsibility for your actions.

No part of this book may be reproduced or transmitted in any form or by any means whatsoever without written permission from the author, except in the case of brief quotations to be used in critical articles and reviews.

Editor: Rusti L Lehay
Cover design and typesetting: Teena Clipston
Illustrations: Robert Allan

Printed in Australia

In Memory

Of my mother and my grandfather, both of whom had to live their last days in a nursing home diagnosed with illnesses that included the symptoms of memory impairment.

Dedicated

To Joany Hanson, whom I met at MindValley University in Croatia, and who set me on the path to write this book.

To my husband Robert and our children, Mollie and James, for the support and encouragement throughout the writing of this book.

To the Townsville Good Shepherd Nursing Home staff, residents and relatives for their stories, experiences and insights... some that I have shared in this book.

CONTENTS

Ten concepts for visiting a relative with dementia 06
Foreword 07
Chapter One: Why visit if they don't know who I am? 09
                Let me introduce myself 11
                Communication 12
                Letters/cards 13
                Using the phone 13
                Skype 15
                Face to face 16
                A visiting template 18
                Christine Bryden 21
                Diaries 23
Chapter Two: Activities, through the 5 senses 25
                What activities can I do? 26
                Smell 27
                Sight 28
                Hearing 28
                Touch 29
                Pets 30
                Fiddle blanket 31
                Doll therapy 32
                Taste 33
                Children 33
                General activities 35
Chapter Three: Testing their memory 37
                Quizzing 38
Chapter Four: Reality versus distraction 41
                Story 42
Chapter Five: So how did my visit help? 49
                Your visit 50
                Support 51
                Golden rules 51
                My final story is Pumpa's story 53
Interesting Facts: Myths and misinformation 55
Resources 61

Ten concepts for visiting a relative with dementia who no longer recognises you

1. Live in the moment they are in.
2. When you argue with or correct them – nobody wins.
3. Your mission is to spend quality time together.
4. They may swing in and out of lucidity – they are not trying to upset you.
5. Take things slowly, remain calm, and happy… breathe and then breathe again.
6. A hug/touch/smile means more than words.
7. Fill your heart with love, then follow it.
8. Be prepared with a back-up plan for your communication.
9. If you start getting upset/angry/frustrated – remove yourself with a smile (there is no shame in leaving earlier than planned).
10. Their reality dictates your actions. Follow their lead.

Foreword

I Don't Know Who You Are, But I Love You *speaks to everyone who has a loved one with dementia and also to the professionals supporting families and visitors in their facilities.*

Nela Allan uses both personal experience and the stories of real people to talk about how engagement, contact and love can help people with dementia and the people who love them. Sharing and offering practical ways in which we can stay engaged, families and visitors will feel empowered and supported.

While science and medicine continues to advance in the development of treatment and research into causes of dementia, it is only a part of the picture. The progress and knowledge gained in continuing human relationships and over-coming isolation are likely to remain at the core of achieving the best quality of life and happiness for dementia sufferers.

I Don't Know Who You Are, But I Love You *is a good humoured and easy to read exploration and guide to dementia for anyone wondering how they can continue to remain connected and be a part of the life of loved ones experiencing dementia.*

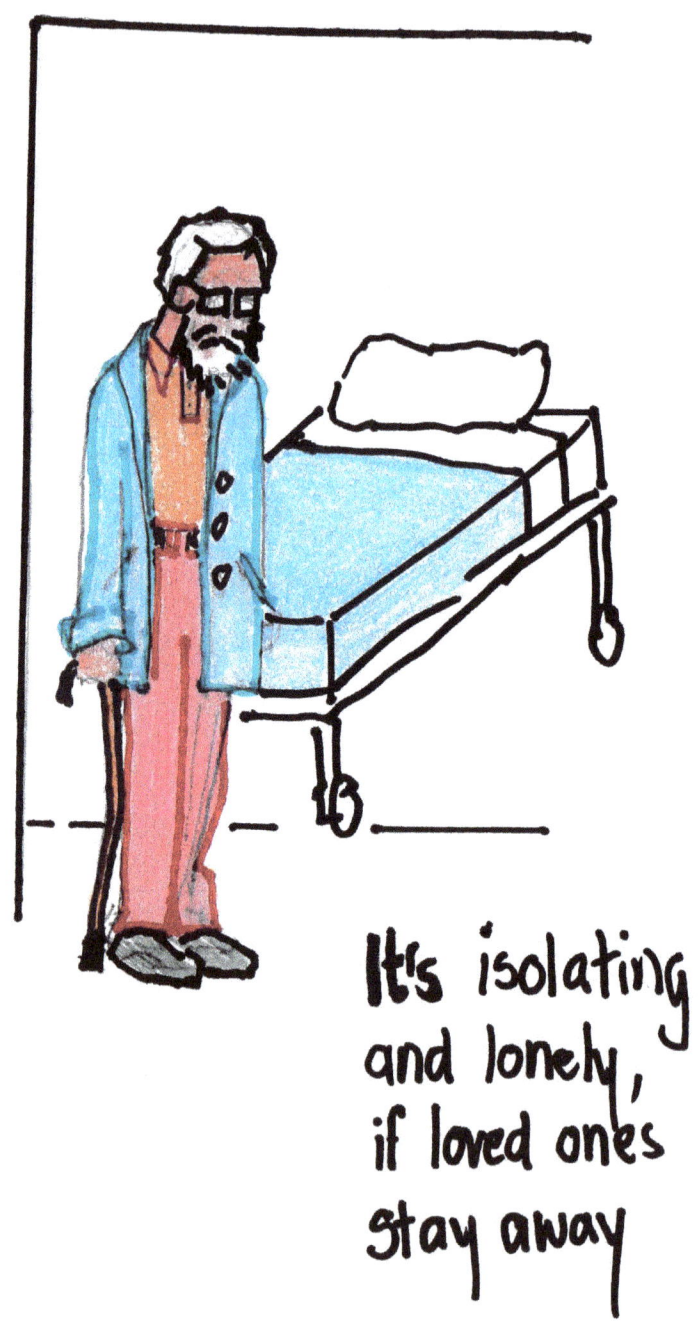

Chapter One

Why visit if they don't know who I am?

Remembering the past and your position in it doesn't really matter. What matters now is being there and having a quality connection in the present moment to create a meaningful experience. Visiting is the most important thing you can do.

Let me introduce myself:

I am a registered nurse and have worked in the Residential Aged Care Industry for over 25 years. Each facility I have worked in had a Dementia Unit – or as I prefer to call them "Memory Support Units" (MSU's). This is an area of the facility that has secured parameters so that the residents are kept safe as they may just walk out and away and keep on walking, not knowing where they are as many have become unaware of dangers such as roads and cars.

I have spent many hours supporting relatives through their visits and counselling them when they encounter troubles, develop concerns or face unwanted behaviours. I have set up support groups for relatives and provided education on how to make it through a visit when they were no longer recognised.

It wasn't until I attended the MindValley University 2019 in Pula, Croatia, that a lady named Joany gave me the idea to write a book. I was talking with a group of people (Joany included) and one of the group was talking about their mother who had dementia. She was not visiting her anymore because her mum didn't know who she was, so she didn't see the point of visiting and felt embarrassed and a bit useless during the visits as she didn't know what to do or say. I asked her to give it another go, told her a few stories, and gave some tips, to which Joany reinforced the idea that a book with my ideas and experience would help many people – so thank you Joany Hanson, here it is.

I am going to be relating my stories and advice around the people who have dementia who are living in a Residential Aged Care Facility and my own experiences with family members, however many of the tips and advice and resources will be useful for those of you who are still caring for your loved one at home.

Communication

One of the hardest things during a visit can be knowing what to say, especially if your loved one is unable to remember who you are or anything that happened in the last 20 years. Let me reassure you it is worth it for both of you to keep persisting.

During the course of their dementia, communication can become very difficult. Communication can be good some days and virtually non-existent on others. There are many reasons: they get overtired; they're in pain; or they have an infection. It may be their dementia is progressing and changing your communication style will help to keep communication flowing – it is very important to try everything. Just because your loved one is unable to communicate does not mean they don't want to. They are still there.

If there was a bond between you prior to the onset of dementia, then the bond will still be there – you may just have to redefine it. By this I mean to change the boundaries. For instance, if the loved one is a parent then the boundary of parent /child will no longer exist at this time and a new type of relationship will have to be developed. It might mean acting the part of a general family member, sibling or friend – or get to know them all over again, in a different way – work out what you have in common, and you will, hopefully, know where to start as you know their history, their likes and dislikes. Be prepared for these to change a little as what they enjoyed as a mother/father will be very different to what they enjoyed as a single person.

Let's not get too far ahead of ourselves, I will start by looking at the different forms of communication:

Letters/cards

These are always nice to receive and keep, especially this generation, even if they are unable to read, to have the letters read to them is usually a pleasure. The tip here is to keep it short, write in almost dot point, it is not the length of the letter that is important. Postcards and greetings cards are great because they also have a visual picture that can be used to assist conversations.

Using the phone

I had been working in this industry for about 15 years when my mother was diagnosed with Vascular dementia. I knew something was up long before this as our phone conversations had been getting increasingly awkward. I live in Australia and mum lived in England so I didn't get to see her, which would have been much easier for both of us. My regular phone calls became less regular and I relied more and more upon my siblings for updates on how she was doing.

Because I work with people living with dementia and memory impairment, I was able to structure my conversations with mum to talk about things she could remember. Using prompts that reached her memories, like, "Where did you go to school," or "Where did you live when you first left home?" then I didn't have to manage the conversation. This also helped me fill in a bit of family history, when she shared stories that I had not heard before. So it was a lovely time. My phone calls would start with, "Hi mum it's Nela, your favourite child, what have you been up to today?" I believe it is important to provide a few facts in my opening sentence so mum had a few clues as to who she was talking to. This would also give me an idea of where she was up to with her memory. Some days were good and we talked for a long time, others I just felt it was the most loving thing to do to end the conversation and ring another time.

In one of our last conversations for example, she was telling me about how awful the nuns were at the Catholic school she went to, one nun in particular. Thinking it was time for me to say something, I asked her if she had a lot of trouble with that nun and she replied, "What nun?"

Me: "You know the nun from your school."

Mum: "Oh I don't think there were any nuns at my school."

Me: "Yes mum, you went to a catholic school."

Mum "Did I? Are you sure?"

She had clearly forgotten. She had also forgotten I was on the phone as she had switched on the TV. I ended the conversation not long after.

We had a few more phone calls after this but it was clear she did not remember me and talking about other things was not holding her interest. Silence, which is sometimes easier to do when you are face-to-face, is near to impossible on the phone. On one call, she thought she was hearing voices and once again had forgotten I was on the phone with her.

Skype

We also tried Skype, supported by my sister who sat with mum and set the computer up. This I felt went really well but alas, mum felt it was very confusing and the short time lapse between me speaking and her hearing me speak was difficult for her to comprehend – Although mum did have a computer for many years (long before she got any symptoms of dementia) she was always technophobic. Emails were a struggle, she was constantly deleting things by accident and she even managed to delete the entire Outlook program. So I guess it was not surprising when Skype did not work for us.

Technology was not really an option for my mum but if you are not living nearby, Skype or any one of the other options listed below might be an option for you, especially in the earlier days of the disease. Certainly the visual gives you more topics to talk about if an awkward silence develops, like what colour shirt they are wearing – or some picture in the background. It is definitely worth trying if only to rule it out.

Technology has come a long way since my attempt with Skype and other options are now available like Zoom or Citrix, Facetime Messenger, Whatsapp, where visual conversations can all be had on your smartphone.

Face to face

This option is always the best whenever possible, as we know actually being there is the whole package and uses all our senses. I will be providing examples and discussing each of the senses and how they may aid in easing your visits. In later chapters, I will be describing activities linked to the senses, that can be beneficial for your loved one.

I have found that coming prepared with a few activities, such as handwork for you or ideas for both of you to do together or independently is a great way to have a successful visit.

You are better able to judge what is happening with your loved one when you are face to face and are able to adapt your responses which helps guide the conversation much more easily. Statistics say that 55% of all communication is body language and your loved one is relying heavily on body language to gauge if many of their interactions and greetings are spot on. They can then relax and know they are doing all right. It is important that you are showing open and relaxed body language – smiling is always a winner.

You have more options too, whether you sit, stand, dance or walk, whether you are chatty, quiet, singing or listening to music, whether you are doing an activity with them, assisting them or doing your own thing.

When speaking, I have found it best to use a lower tone as this is more relaxing. Offer small pieces of information at a time allowing them time to process what you have said. Be prepared to become comfortable with silence. 38% of communication relies on the tone and pitch of your voice, again giving your loved one more clues on what is going on. Finally, 7% of communication is on the actual words you use, so what you say is not as important as how you say it and whether your body language matches your tone.

Miss S brought all the ingredients for baking a cake, which her mother used to love to do. She happily set about telling her mother what to do and how to do it, however Miss S did not leave time in between each task instruction, which would have allowed her mother to absorb the information and then follow the instructions. Mrs S became overwhelmed, so she started moving things around, which began to annoy Miss S who was starting to lose control of the activity. The activity ended with Mrs S throwing eggs and sugar at her daughter. Staff stepped in and distracted Mrs S with some of her favorite music. Miss S was assisted with the clean up and gentle suggestions that the activity might have had too many steps. Next time Miss S can either do the activity side-by-side or do some of the steps and give her mother the spoon to do the mixing. Once the mess was cleaned up, she rejoined her mother singing to the music they both loved.

A visiting template

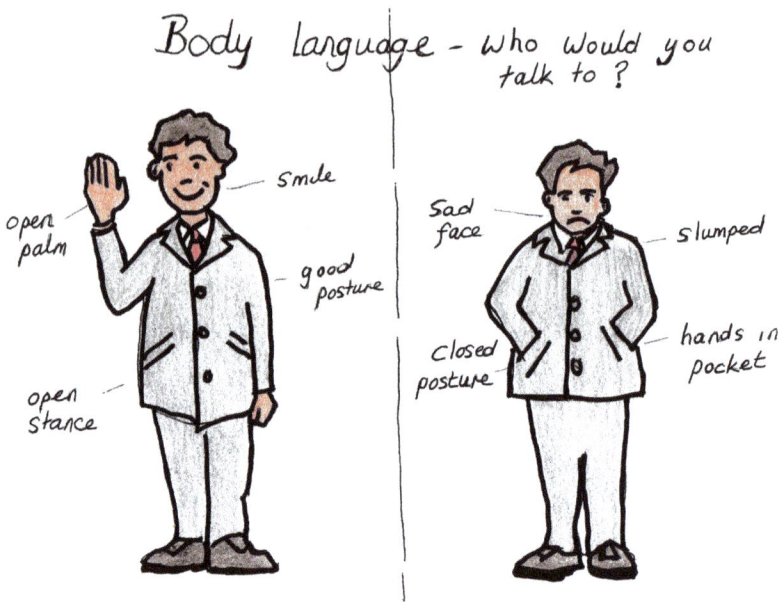

When first seeing the person you are visiting: walk up to them, establish eye contact and hold it if you can, as you introduce yourself. This shows them that you are speaking to them. I have often seen a visitor walk into an MSU saying 'Hi Mum" and several of the residents answer believing the visitor belongs to them.

> **TAKE HOME:**
>
> - Try all forms of communication
> - Phone calls may not be the best form of communication
> - There is no one size fit all answers – everyone is different
> - What works for you on one occasion may not work the next – try everything
> - 55% of communication is body language
> - Be flexible
> - Don't give up

When introducing yourself, use the name they would usually call you and what you are to them – daughter, friend from school, neighbour etc.

A smile is worth a hundred words and can ease many an awkward situation. Look for a quiet space to sit as you talk, away from distracting noises like the TV and other people. This reduces the distractions and makes it easier for them to concentrate on what you are saying and any non-verbal clues you are giving out. It also makes it easier for your loved one as you will not be moving around. I see the resident losing focus when a visitor talks whilst moving around – like making their bed or arranging an activity to do, so save your conversation for when you are still.

Keep your sentences short. If you go on too long, they will have forgotten what you started with – I have to say this happens to me a lot as it does with my colleagues and perhaps you have found this happens to you too. We lead busy lives and can lose focus very easily – like walking into a room and forgetting why you entered it.

Give as many clues as possible, like pointing to something you are talking about, or putting your hand up to your mouth to indicate that what they have is edible.

You do not have to fill all the silences with chatter. It is completely acceptable to sit quietly with them and enjoy just being in each other's company.

Being comfortable with silence is difficult for some people, especially those that love to talk. One visitor, Mr K, was such a person. For these people, bringing along something to do to occupy the mind is an easy way to do silence. I personally found him very relaxing as I did not have to contribute to the conversation, as he was happy to just chat away for hours. However his wife's experience was completely different. She would look at him with what I can only describe as a startled look, then she would start fidgeting, looking around nervously working herself up until she would shout at the top of her lungs, "SHUT UP," and storm off to her room refusing to come out. Mr K often seemed oblivious to the stress that he had caused his wife. We intervened and explained the situation. We did some inquiries and found out he enjoyed crossword puzzles. The next visit we watched and when we saw that she was starting to fidget, we sent him a text message. When his phone beeped, he stopped talking and took out his crossword book. His silence calmed her down and they sat together quite contentedly for the rest of his visit.

Other relatives who feel awkward just sitting quietly for a visit opt to take their loved ones for a walk, (often using a wheelchair) as this gives both a break and a change of scenery can be very welcome. Many partners bring something to do as their loved one can no longer converse or do activities, however, just sitting reading a book or knitting keeps you occupied and being close to your loved one makes a difference to them. People can definitely sense someone who cares for them being there, as they are far more relaxed and for long after the visitor has left, staff report a noticeable difference in the person. A new shift of nurses will come on and they instantly know the resident had a visitor by the demeanour of the resident.

Come prepared with things to do, conversations to have and a flexible attitude.

Christine Bryden

Christine Bryden is a lady who developed Early Onset Dementia at the tender age of 46. This early onset dementia is an uncommon form of Alzheimers accounting for only 5-10 percent of all Alzheimer cases. Christine has been a great resource for learning about what it is like to have dementia and what things are helpful and what are not. I have included a link here for one of the many YouTube videos that Christine has created – the one cited below was developed in conjunction with the Australian Aged Care Channel – a learning platform for staff working in the industry. It is definitely useful for anyone looking after a relative with Dementia. https://tinyurl.com/y6nvnbnw

I have found her videos extremely useful in understanding what a person with dementia is going through. By just putting

Christine's name into a search engine like Google you will find many other useful videos.

Christine has a very supportive husband who patiently labelled everything with what it is, when they brought it, why it is important. They had a daily routine diary, so Christine could check things off that she needed to do and know what was happening next.

Two decades on, Christine has progressed in her dementia but is still sharing her knowledge of what it is like from the inside perspective – something her doctors are amazed at because they predicted she would only have 18 months to live.

Diaries

Many families find it helpful to keep a diary with their loved one, showing the dates of their visits, what they did and the date of the next visit. The resident can then look to see when someone last came to visit them.

Mrs J complained daily that nobody ever visited her. Her family, who visited nearly every day, brought a diary and made a habit of going to it first thing and asking her: "Now, what did we do last time?" This gives them a bit of focus, a discussion point and proof that they did visit not so long ago without having to say it. It became a ritual and settled Mrs J down when she was feeling lonely. Staff would say, "Let's look at the diary and see who your last visitor was and what you did." Eventually Mrs J began carrying her diary around and showing other residents, appearing very proud that she had had visitors.

TAKE HOME:

- Establish eye contact
- Find a quiet place
- Stand/sit still when talking
- Keep sentences short
- Come prepared with things to talk about and do
- Silence can be the best activity of all

24 - Nela Allan

Chapter Two

Activities, through the 5 senses

We learn to focus, experience life, grow and communicate through our five senses. Mindfulness begins when we pay attention to what is happening around us.

What activities can I do?

The possibilities are endless. I have chosen to divide the types of activities you could use by going through the five senses. Whatever you decide will depend on the abilities of your loved one and you might like to discuss this with the staff as they might have some suggestions that could help. Keep their interests and past profession in mind when selecting activities as they will work best if they are meaningful for your loved one. Do not worry if you think the activities are too simple or childish.

I looked after a lovely lady who would spend her days sorting a mixture of coloured beads into their same coloured cups. This one day she appeared much more talkative and I asked her if she would like something a bit more meaningful to do. She replied, "No thank you, I tried that once but I could not manage the task most days and that made me feel stupid. I know that I can do this task even on my worst day, so while I can still do this, it is what I want to do. It makes me feel successful."

Before starting an activity, always invite your loved one to join in; offering this choice helps them feel in control. Match your speed with the pace of their speech and actions. This may take a bit of patience. Stay strong.

If your loved one wants to join in but is failing at the tasks, then just get them to hold something – be encouraging. If things don't proceed as you planned or hoped, laugh it off. Laughter shows that it really doesn't matter. After all, it is about the connection between the two of you, not the task that is important.

Don't talk too much when getting the activity up and running – a demonstration will be far more effective, then give simple choices as you progress through the activity.

Simple activities are the best, as too much information gets confusing. Take your time and give your loved one a chance to process what you have said and enough time for them to form an answer. Slow and steady is the way ahead.

Smell:

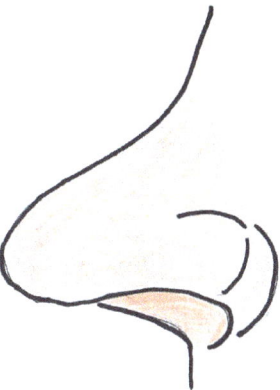

The sense of smell triggers the memory better than any other sense. Lily of the Valley reminds me of my mother as she always used talcum powder with that fragrance, my Grandmother always used Ponds face cream, my grandfather – old spice… you get the idea. These fragrances bring up very strong memories for me of each person.

If you are able to, take a few fragrances with you that you think may spark a memory, like taking a sprig of Rosemary, telling them what it is, and getting them to smell it and see what they think of the smell. If nothing comes to mind, it is still a nice activity – providing you pick items that smell nice. This can be an aftershave or perfume that they or their partner used. It can be bringing in a favourite meal, (checking with staff first that this is ok). Or even seeing if you are able to cook something with your loved one at the facility.

Many Aged Care places have a sensory garden that can be used if you have not brought anything with you. This activity, combined with a walk outside, is a popular thing to do.

Sight:

Photographs are great, especially those of when your loved one was younger. I have seen 'talking' photo albums – where you can record who is in the picture and what they were to your loved one. This recording plays as the page is turned – this is also especially nice for the days when you are unable to visit.

Anything visual is recommended as we tend to believe our eyes more than any other sense. Remember 55% of communication is body language – this includes other visual clues.

A visual option always available is walking outside and looking at the gardens, colours, birds, butterflies, or children (if you bring yours with you).

Games like cards or scrabble are very popular, anything that they used to play. Noughts and crosses (tic tac toe) is another easy game that does not take a lot of concentration but is extremely popular and I spy are useful ones if you have forgotten to bring something with you.

Magazines, colouring in books, bringing in a laptop and watching a movie are all good visual activities.

Hearing:

The sound of your voice is something they may remember and gives clues as to who you are. Together with all the other senses, it helps your loved one make sense of the world around them.

Music can be very uplifting or relaxing and singing along to favourite tunes is a great activity. Getting up and dancing/swaying to the music, or if they are unable, then just tapping out the rhythm.

Try reading a book or magazine articles out loud. Look at pictures. Telling jokes – let's face it, laughter is the best medicine for everyone and can leave you with a lovely warm memory of the day.

Below are two YouTube videos about singing with a resident who has Dementia – be warned and have a box of tissues handy when you watch them. They show the power of music and singing to a resident and how it can bring them back to life. There are many more available, however, these two are my favourites.
https://tinyurl.com/bfg6bxg
https://tinyurl.com/jgvd2cx

Touch:

One of our very basic needs is contact with others. As humans, we can be fed and watered but without touch we fail to thrive. I also believe, people with dementia are always in need of more touch. This can be so healing and restorative to relationships. Be careful and let your loved one guide what kind of touch is comfortable for them.

Even before they are diagnosed, a person will tend to start isolating themselves, as they know something is wrong. They will start to limit the amount of time they put themselves in positions where they may fail. Instead of going out to the shops where they might meet people they have forgotten or forget why they went out, or not recognise the money in their purse, they prefer to stay home where they will not be embarrassed.

It is very typical that a person will hand over the jobs of shopping or cooking or the finances to their partner as they can no longer remember how to do it. They don't visit their friends as they can't remember their names or some of the stories that they tell. By distancing themselves from people they rob themselves of touch.

Holding a hand, giving a hand massage, a manicure or a shoulder massage are all great things to do. Hair brushing, oh, this is my favourite. I would happily sit for hours if someone is playing with my hair. It is a lovely sensation and I would actually do the same for a hand or foot massage too.

Pets:

If you have a family pet, then bringing them in for a visit can be very soothing though you must check with the facility first as pets can be overwhelmed by the residents who might flock around trying to pat them. This has led to residents being bitten before. The way around this is to have your relative brought out to a certain area where they alone can come and enjoy the family pet.

You can purchase a toy cat or dog that looks and behaves like

a real cat or dog. The cats can stretch and purr, the dogs move their heads up and down and their fur is very soft and tactile. They can be placed on a lap where the resident can pat them. Showing love and tenderness to another gives a sense of belonging and being needed.

Fiddle blankets:

Some residents can become very restless and agitated and finding the cause of this is important, especially if it is caused by pain. One common cause is boredom and therefore activities become vital in this person's life. Fiddle blankets are great for residents who are always wanting to keep busy. These fiddle blankets can have locks and keys, zips, pockets, bells, buttons and buttonholes, ribbons all knotted up (to be undone) and so on.

I have seen families set up a handbag full of things for a female relative and fiddle boxes for males. These have been extremely successful.

Mr F was a carpenter and his family set up a box with a tape measure, pencil and notebook, some different size pieces of wood, a spirit level and a ruler, Mr F would happily go around the facility measuring things up, jotting down things in his notebook and designing tables and benches.

Doll therapy:

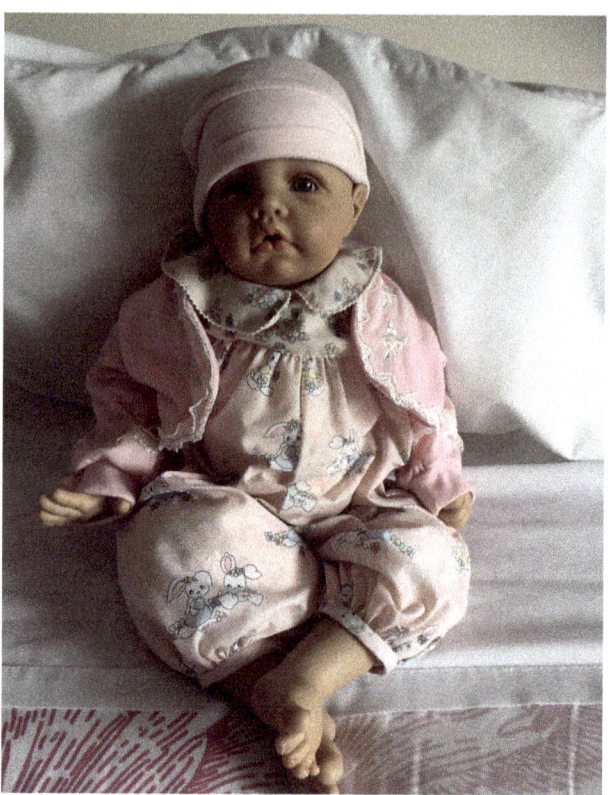

Doll therapy is another very useful tool for some residents. This doll is identical in looks and weight to a real baby. Some models even cry. We had a resident that went everywhere with her doll baby and would not eat until she had fed the baby first. It slept next to her bed in a specially made cot. She loved this baby and felt so proud when anyone came over and commented on how beautiful she was and asked if they could cuddle her.

Others, of course, will say they don't play with dolls and be a little insulted that you have suggested it.

When using doll therapy it is best to leave the doll laying in a comfortable looking position and see if your loved one goes to pick it up, rather than offering them the baby to hold. The same thing is true for a real baby. It has to be when your loved one is feeling the desire to interact on their own.

Taste:

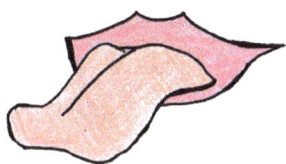

Going out for a cuppa and cake is a perfect activity. If unable to leave the facility – or you do not feel comfortable doing this, then you can have a cuppa and cake in the facility, bringing your own favourite cakes in. Again check with the facility. It doesn't have to be cakes, it could be savoury snacks, hot or cold dishes, chocolates, fruit or a range of all of these. Receiving a gift like this is a treat for everyone involved. Sharing a food is sharing an experience that can be bonding without being threatening. I have found with many residents who suffer from dementia, that finger foods are often best - easier to manage and don't interrupt their meal times and routines.

Children:

Many years ago, I had just had my second child. The local college rang me, urgently needing someone to do the assessments for a group of students doing the certificate 111 in aged care. The students were doing their practical experience in a nursing home. I told them I had just had a baby, to which they responded, "Bring him with you," so I did.

One of the students I was to assess was in an MSU assisting a resident (with Dementia) to eat. The gentleman was a very tall and heavy-set man who had been there for several years, had never spoken and although the staff had tried many things, he had never reacted to any activity. I walked in with my son in my arms, the gentleman looked up, smiled and put his arms out to hold the baby.

I have to say I was very nervous as I did not know this man, but something in his smile was so loving and gentle that I gave him my baby to hold and nervously watched as he sat back down.

He cuddled my son, gently rocking him, then he started singing a lullaby in the most beautiful voice. I was extremely relieved and as I looked around at the rest of the room, the entire place had stopped in amazement and some staff were crying, saying that they had never seen him like this and how wonderful it was to see him so happy. The staff immediately started chattering excitedly and arranging to get one of their therapy dolls assigned to this gentleman.

This scenario is not unusual and I often see children providing a source of great joy, so if you have children, please bring them with you. If you are nervous of some of the other residents in the unit, who can make funny noises, or invade your personal boundaries, you can ask the staff if there is a room or area you can go to that is a bit more private. They will be happy to help as your loved one is much happier during and after a visit.

Bring things for the children to do, like a colouring book or a card game as when your conversation slows down or stops you can both just watch the children play. This is an activity by itself that can be very enjoyable. It keeps the children happy – preventing boredom and just having the children and you near is what is important for your loved one.

General activities

Other activities that fit into several of the senses can be something related to your loved one's profession, i.e. if they were an accountant then you could bring in some business figures for them to add up, an engineer/construction/carpenter, you could bring in a tape measure and they could measure up an area of the building. A gardener could grow some vegetables or herbs in a window box or pot plants.

TAKE HOME:

- Go up to the person you are visiting before speaking
- Introduce yourself by name and who you are
- Minimise distractions (turn off TV)
- Smile
- Use the 5 senses to prepare activities
- Be flexible, go with the flow your loved one is in
- It is good for children to connect with their relative
- Bring activities for the children to do
- Ask for a quiet area away from the other residents

Chapter Three

Testing their memory

Challenging a person is putting someone on the spot and can lead to panic, withdrawal or a defensive outburst.

Testing their memory

I would love to have a dollar for every time I heard someone ask, "Do you know who I am?" to a person suffering with Dementia. Occasionally they will get it right, but more often than not this question will make them feel inadequate and frustrated.

People who have been diagnosed with Dementia have memory loss. They are not stupid. They know they should know, they just can't remember. This is very frustrating and scary for them not to mention embarrassing – just as you get embarrassed when you meet someone in the street that you recognise but can't recall their name or where you met them. Challenging them does not magically make it all better.

Quizzing

We, I am sure, have all had times when we have forgotten how to spell simple words like 'their' or can't recall the name of an item like a pen saying things like "can you pass the... thingy, you know the....the... the pen," we eventually remember.

A person with Dementia will have the same problems with the outcome that they do not remember. So if you challenge them by asking them what a certain item is called, like holding up a pen – "what is this called?" or "do you remember when?" your loved one will not hear anything after that initial question as they will be trying to find an answer that will make you stop asking them things without getting it WRONG. They know that they should know the answer and the frustration, embarrasment and feeling stupid is less than helpful to creating a successful visit. Remember the wisdom of silence. That can be your surest way to a win-win scenario. Some will react defensively, some will become visibly upset, some will just shrug, but I am sure all will feel inadequate.

There is no point to testing a person's memory when they have Dementia as their short and long term recall can change from moment to moment.

Far better to say "Look at this pen." Or, "This is one of my memories with you." Or just sitting next to them, maybe holding hands, and just enjoying the company. Mrs V who came in daily to visit her husband told me that she used to feel she had to entertain him when she visited, but became exhausted with this. When she realised he did not seem to care too much if she was just quiet, she then remembered when they were at home together all he did was sit in a chair next to her and only became agitated if she moved away. She now brings in a few edible treats for them both, her knitting, a good book and holds his hand every now and then but just gets on with her own thing.

So, share your memories instead of asking questions.

TAKE HOME:

- Give as many clues as possible
- Don't challenge their memory
- Be in their time zone
- Share your stories

Remember

Your loved one who has dementia is not GIVING you a hard time.

Because of dementia they are HAVING a hard time.

Chapter Four

Reality versus distraction

The more prepared you are for a visit, the easier it will be. Remember: Prior preparation prevents poor performance.

Story

Mrs G went to the MSU to visit her husband, which she did several times a week. This time, as usual, she introduced herself and said who she was and they chatted and laughed, then Mr G said, "You are a really beautiful, fun person, but you are not my wife." Mrs G was devastated and felt heartbroken as this was the first time that he had not recognised her.

Some visits are tough and I wish there was a magic wand around to help people. Alas there is not, just the knowledge that this is not them, they are not doing it intentionally and the difficulties you are experiencing are due to the disease.

Now we may have to introduce ourselves by our name and say we are family and leave it at that, so we can have a comfortable visit without sparking any potentially hurtful comments. They are not meant to be hurtful. It is your loved one trying to make sense of the information they have with a failing memory.

Behaviours

Forgetting things is not done on purpose – though it does seem like it when they have lucid moments.

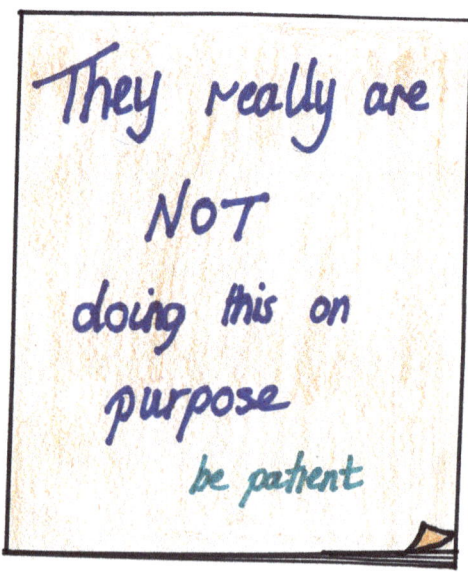

On some days it really feels like they are playing you for a fool and very conveniently forgetting things and then very pointedly remembering them.

This really is not done on purpose and can be just as frustrating for them. Just like in an earlier chapter when my mum did not remember the story she had just told me minutes before about the nun. It is one of the stages of Dementia and is very common.

Important: It is probably timely to mention that not all people diagnosed with dementia experience the same things. Some will have strange behaviours, some may be verbally aggressive, others may be physically aggressive, some are sweet natured and so on. It will depend on many things, not least of which is the type of dementia they have – if you are unsure then it is best to contact their Doctor. If in a residential aged care facility, then ask to talk with the Clinical Nurse to develop a better understanding of the individual issues with your loved one and some personalised tips on how to have a smooth visit that doesn't leave either party feeling upset. Although I will not be covering behaviours in this book, there are many resources out there for how to handle difficult or unwelcome behaviours such as https://tinyurl.com/y2lng3vl or https://www.alzheimers.org.uk/ or https://alzfdn.org/ Nearly every country has a dementia support organisation that will have useful information on behaviours and suggestions on what to do or where to get more information.

The frustrating thing about sudden clarity of memory is that it could last only for moments, days or even weeks. It may happen hourly, daily, weekly or longer. There is no pattern that can be determined and you never know when it is going to happen. This can be very stressful. Please try to remember it is not personal (even if it feels like it or seems to be directed at you). If you get upset, sad or angry, please try and walk away. When you go back even after a short interval, they may have forgotten and your visit can continue, or you may have to leave it for another day.

If they do remember things, go with it and be happy they are remembering. You can see if they remember other things by sharing one of your favourite memories. These moments may be rare, and hanging on to the treasure of lucid moments can help you through the tough times. These moments can also be very tiring as their memory can flicker on and off quite rapidly leaving you feeling exhausted – this is also exhausting for them.

They may express this exhaustion through anger. Sometimes the best way to deal with this is to sit quietly with them, take a deep breath and relax. Be gentle with yourself, remembering there is always the option of a fresh visit on another day.

The best way to communicate is to give as many clues as possible without overloading them with information – it's a balancing act.

Remember my opening sentence? I gave my name, *(Nela)* who I am to them *(your favourite child)* and seeing what they remember – if anything *(what have you been up to today?)*

For them: They will know what to call you and who you are, giving them a way they can react to you.

For you: This gives you an idea of how their memory is at this moment in time, without being confrontational. They may say "I don't know" or they may tell you what they would like to have been doing or what they actually have done. Giving you vital clues as to how to continue the conversation.

TAKE HOME:

- Check with the nurse or doctor about diagnosis and what is involved
- Walk away if you are getting upset
- Sit quietly – enjoy the company
- End the visit gently if they are getting upset

Reality versus distraction

Sometimes it is best, (unless directed otherwise by a Doctor or Nurse), to be in the reality that they are in. In one of the facilities I worked in, there was a lady, Joan, whose husband had died 17 years prior to her coming into the facility. A dear friend, Annie visited Joan every day and always left because she couldn't bear to see Joan crying, which she did during every visit. One day I managed to catch up to Annie and ask her what she thought was the cause of Joan's tears. Anne told me, "She asks about her husband and each time I have to tell her, he has died." Through these visits by her devoted friend, Joan daily found out that her husband had died and each time it was like hearing the news for the first time.

After sharing my thoughts with Annie, her next visit went really well, they had a few laughs and parted happily. Annie just said, "I have no idea where he is," when asked the same question. She had brought in a picture of Joan's husband when he was younger and one of their wedding and said, "Doesn't he look handsome in this picture?" and the conversation continued happily and I believe every visit from then on. The use of the photo to distract Joan allowed the conversation to go in a different direction helping both of them.

Where is Bob?

OK

In this instance, and many others, I have found it much better to not tell the whole truth (and sometimes telling a little white lie) so the person with memory loss does not have to relive painful memories over and over.

On the flip side of this we looked after a lady, Mavis. Again her husband had also died many years earlier but when Mavis asked where her husband was, if you told her you didn't know where he was she would increasingly get more and more agitated, pace up and down and eventually get angry. Here, we found it worked well to tell Mavis the truth, that he had been unwell for some time and had died several years ago. In response to this, Mavis would say, "Oh, okay" and go happily about her day.

It really is a matter of seeing how each person reacts and adjust your conversation accordingly. The best thing for all concerned when in relationship with a person living with Dementia is to learn what is potentially upsetting and ask for help when you need to explore alternatives. Like Annie needing to tell a little white lie which let their visits continue on a positive note for them both.

I am not an advocate of lying but am more opposed to causing grief and upset when there is no point to it. If unsure what to say, remember the staff are there to help and they may have discovered what works best or have a method already in place that has proved helpful. In such scenarios, consistency can be most helpful.

TAKE HOME:

- Distracting the conversation to avoid grief is the nicer option
- A little white lie may help your loved one remain calm and happy
- Ask a doctor or nurse the best way to handle a situation
- Consistency with information is key
- When situations change, change with them

Chapter Five

So how did my visit help?

Visiting your loved one is a time for you to build some lovely memories of how you supported your loved one through a very difficult time in their lives. This can be comforting to you, knowing that your visits gave them a day with love.

Your visit

Whether your visit has gone really well or whether you have had a less than ideal visit, the fact that you were there has a profound effect on your loved one.

Once you have gone home, the staff often report that your loved one has far less behavioural issues and appears far more alert, and is more inclined to join in with other activities.

If asked, they often cannot remember that they had a visitor that day. (This is where a diary can come in handy.) However staff report that they appear much happier. So, your visits make a powerful impact on the life of your loved one even if they can't show it or don't know it.

I have often observed the huge difference a visit makes when residents have had a visitor. I am not sure if it is the one-on-one attention (which, lets face it, everyone loves), the feeling that they are with someone they love or the distraction from their usual routine. All I can tell you is the difference is there, even if your loved one gets frustrated or exhibits some behaviours while you are there, the visit has still made their day a special one.

The person with dementia is living in the now. They are not building memories. They are experiencing things moment by moment.

Although activities are great, being there is more important. It is about being together and in some cases less is best. You don't always have to be doing something.

It's about working out what works, in the sense that your loved one is calm, or engaged, or happy, or all of these things. Look, listen and remember. By going over the visit that you ended early, examine what may have triggered the breakdown in communication and try to avoid the same trap at the next visit.

Support

There are often support groups set up by the facility and if your facility does not have one, then ask if you can start one up. The facility will support this and offer a space where you can meet. In Queensland Australia, the local Dementia Australia office may help you set this up and offer insight into the disease process. If you are technology savvy, then setting up a Facebook group might be helpful and supportive.

Carer groups exist to help people who care for others, giving relatives a bit of time out for themselves as you know, when looking after a loved one, the carer often neglects themselves.

If looking after a loved one at home, there are options like respite care available that will allow you to have a break while your loved one spends a few days in a nursing home.

Golden rules:
- Don't stress
- Minimise distractions
- Keep sentences short
- Involve them in meaningful activities
- Slow down – give them time to understand and respond
- Start with simple tasks making them more complex if suitable
- Face-to-face visits
- Prepare for your visit with things to do
- Touch is important – hold hands/massage/a hug
- Go with the flow
- Talk less, demonstrate more
- When you leave a secure MSU – don't let a resident walk out behind you

My final story is Pumpa's story

Pumpa is the name we gave to my grandpa (the eldest grandchild could not say grandpa – and the name of Pumpa was what all grand and great grandchildren called him.

I had recently been awarded my nursing certificate when my sister and I visited him in the nursing home. My sister did not like visiting the home as it made her nervous with all the funny noises and some of the residents, she felt, were very scary looking, so we mostly went together.

On previous visits, Pumpa had mistaken me for my mother (we do look very much alike) and on occasion would tell me about his daughter and how she also had gone to Australia and did I know her? So we were used to his not really knowing us and being very confused, however Pumpa was a storyteller and would enthral us with his magical stories making our visits very enjoyable.

The last visit I made to Pumpa, he was sitting thoughtfully in a chair. He looked up as we walked in, smiled a beaming smile at us and said, "I don't know who you are, but you must be family because I love you."

TAKE HOME:

- Your loved one lives moment to moment
- Sometimes less is best
- Look for triggers that may cause the visit to end sooner than planned
- Be there
- When situations change, change with them
- Look after yourself and take time for you

Interesting Facts

Myths and misinformation

There are many myths and misinformation out there around dementia as well as a lot of confusion. Many do not realise that it is a terminal progressive illness. There is a lot of exciting research that hints at a cure being close, however, at this point there is no cure.

56 - Nela Allan

Early signs of dementia:

Progressive and frequent memory loss

Confusion

Personality change

Apathy and withdrawal

Loss of ability to perform everyday tasks.

Dementia is a terminal illness

Dementia is used to describe loss of memory, intellect, rationality

Dementia is more prominent in women and is the leading cause of death in women

A person with dementia still has a sense of humour – laughter is great therapy

Dementia is NOT a normal part of aging

We are motivated by things we enjoy – so are they

A person with dementia responds well to music

A person with dementia still needs hugs and love from family and friends

Experiencing loss and grief when a loved one has dementia is normal

Dementia has 7 stages

Independence is kept through different and meaningful activities

Dementia is a progressive illness

Resources

*There are many resources available.
Here are a few to get you started:*

**Alzheimer's Australia offers a National Dementia Hotline:
1 800 100-500**
Website: www.alzheimers.org.au

My Aged care portal – to access respite care,
aged care packages or aged care facility:
www.careabout.com.au

Dementia Australia:
www.dementia.org.au

Carers Australia:
www.carersaustralia.com.au

I hope this has been helpful and will allow you to visit with your loved one in a way that brings you both joy. It is a difficult time for everyone so we must try and remember that under all the frustration and memory loss, there is still a person who may not know who you are but their whole being remembers that they love you, even if they can't tell you that.

- Nela Allan

www.ingramcontent.com/pod-product-compliance
Lightning Source LLC
LaVergne TN
LVHW010308070426
835510LV00025B/3416